Australia

Kate Turner

Elaine Stratford and Joseph Powell, Consultants

NATIONAL GEOGRAPHIC

WASHINGTON, D.C.

Contents

Foreword

For countless centuries, Australia managed to hide its secrets from the rest of the world. When the first European settlers arrived, some of them realized at once that they had encountered a kind of scientific paradise. Australia's original peoples had already unlocked a number of the deepest mysteries of the bizarre vegetation, birds, and animals. Ordinary settlers did their best to make a living from strange environments. They made appalling mistakes, and probably would have made far fewer had they bothered to make close friends with the native peoples. Even so, their farming systems quickly created extensive new landscapes which reshaped the appearance of the country. Australians put huge brain and muscle power into mining mineral wealth and creating great national parks, big cities, and small settlements. Much of Australia's history of pioneering achievement in science and technology stems from the search for ways of wresting a living from unfamiliar territory. And the history of its contribution to art, literature, poetry, and music is also entwined with landscape creation.

If landscapes are documents, they are not easily read without some relevant background in history and geography. This book aims to provide some of that background. Australia was also "the land of the second chance"—a kind of social laboratory in which great ideals were officially approved, not just debated. These included pioneering laws for "a fair day's pay for a fair day's work;" free, compulsory state education; and voting rights for all adults, including women.

The environmental-social experiment continued. Originally jealously protective of a largely Anglo-Celtic heritage, Australians came to accept increasing numbers of immigrants from southern Europe, then from Asia and

elsewhere. Occasionally, suburban mosques, temples and shrines remind casual visitors to ignore the lazy stereotyping of modern Australia. The busy street presence of immigrants from China, Vietnam, Cambodia, and Laos, and more recently from India, emphasizes Australia's growing diversity.

Australia remains a treasure trove for the natural scientist, but it is also a Mecca for ecological tourists and a surprise for casual visitors. Read on to discover more about the Australian experiment with an ancient, secret land.

▲ **An aboriginal man leans on his fishing spear at Kakadu National Park in the Northern Territory.**

J. Powell.

Joseph Powell,
Monash University,
Melbourne, Australia

Land
of the
Big Red
Desert

AT THE HEART OF AUSTRALIA lies the largest rock in the world. Uluru rises like a whale's back from a flat red-soil desert called the Red Center. The Aboriginal people, Australia's indigenous population, believe Uluru is sacred. The rock is 1,100 feet (335 m) high, and has pathways to the top. In 1985 the land was returned to its traditional owners, the Pitjantjatjara, who are one of the hundreds of different Aboriginal groups in Australia. The Pitjantjatjara leased it back to the government as a national park, although they prefer people to see the rock from the ground rather than climbing on their sacred site. The landscapes of Australia's interior are often dry and barren, but the Aboriginal people believe that many landscape features have spiritual meaning.

◀ **It is easy to see why Uluru is sacred to the Pitjantjatjara. Its sandstone changes color in different lights: at sunset it glows a fiery orange-red.**

At a Glance

WHAT'S THE WEATHER LIKE?

Australia has variable rainfall. Much of the interior gets less than 10 inches (25 cm) of rain a year, and has frequent droughts, while parts of the coast receive a lot of rain. Temperatures often soar above 100° F (38° C) in the summer (December to February in the Southern Hemisphere), except in Tasmania, where the climate is much cooler. The map opposite shows the physical features of Australia. Labels on this map and on similar maps throughout this book identify most of the places pictured in each chapter.

Average Temperature & Rainfall

Average High/Low Temperatures; Yearly Rainfall

Alice Springs (Central)
83.3° F (28.5° C) / 55.6° F (13.1° C); 11 in (28 cm)

Darwin (North Coast)
89.2° F (31.8° C) / 73.6° F (23.1° C); 69 in (175 cm)

Sydney (Southeast Coast)
70.7° F (21.5° C) / 56.5° F (13.6° C); 48 in (122 cm)

Adelaide (South Coast)
71.6° F (22.0° C) / 53.6° F (12.0° C); 20 in (51 cm)

Perth (Southwest Coast)
73.0° F (23.3° C) / 55.8° F (13.2° C); 34 in (86 cm)

Hobart (Tasmania)
62.1° F (16.7° C) / 46.8° F (8.2° C); 23 in (59 cm)

Fast Facts

OFFICIAL NAME: Commonwealth of Australia

FORM OF GOVERNMENT: Federal Parliamentary Democracy

CAPITAL: Canberra

POPULATION: 20,683,554

OFFICIAL LANGUAGE: English

MONETARY UNIT: Australian dollar

AREA: 2,969,906 square miles (7,692,024 square kilometers)

HIGHEST POINT: Mount Kosciuszko, 7,310 feet (2,228 meters)

LOWEST POINT: Lake Eyre, 52 feet (16 meters) below sea level

MAJOR MOUNTAIN RANGES: Great Dividing Range, Macdonnell Ranges

MAJOR RIVERS: Murray–Darling, Murrumbidgee, Lachlan, Macquarie

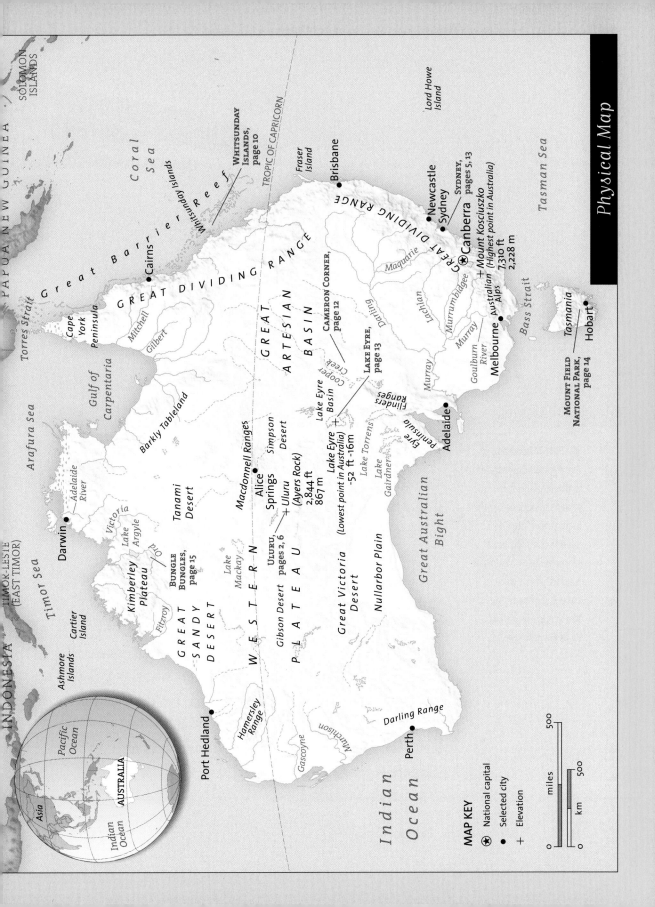

SOLOMON ISLANDS

PAPUA NEW GUINEA

INDONESIA

TIMOR-LESTE (EAST TIMOR)

Coral Sea

Arafura Sea

Timor Sea

Gulf of Carpentaria

Torres Strait

Great Barrier Reef

Whitsunday Islands

WHITSUNDAY ISLANDS, page 10

TROPIC OF CAPRICORN

Cape York Peninsula

Mitchell

Gilbert

Fraser Island

Brisbane

Newcastle

Sydney

SYDNEY, pages 5, 13

Canberra

+ Mount Kosciuszko
7,310 ft
2,228 m (Highest point in Australia)

Lord Howe Island

GREAT DIVIDING RANGE

GREAT DIVIDING RANGE

Cairns

Ashmore Islands

Cartier Island

Darwin

Adelaide River

Victoria

Lake Argyle

Ord

Kimberley Plateau

BUNGLE BUNGLES, page 15

Fitzroy

GREAT SANDY DESERT

Lake Mackay

Tanami Desert

Barkly Tableland

Macdonnell Ranges

Alice Springs

+ Uluru (Ayers Rock)
2,844 ft
867 m

ULURU, pages 2, 6

Simpson Desert

GREAT ARTESIAN BASIN

Cooper Creek

CAMERON CORNER, page 12

Lake Eyre Basin

+ Lake Eyre (Lowest point in Australia)
-52 ft -16m

LAKE EYRE, page 13

Maquarie

Macquarie

Lachlan

Murrumbidgee

Murray

Darling

Murray

Goulburn River

Australian Alps

Melbourne

Bass Strait

Tasmania

MOUNT FIELD NATIONAL PARK, page 14

Hobart

Tasman Sea

Flinders Ranges

Lake Torrens

Lake Gairdner

Eyre Peninsula

Adelaide

Great Australian Bight

Nullarbor Plain

Great Victoria Desert

WESTERN PLATEAU

Gibson Desert

Hamersley Range

Port Hedland

Gascoyne

Murchison

Darling Range

Perth

Indian Ocean

MAP KEY

⊛ National capital
• Selected city
+ Elevation

miles
0   500

km
0   500

Pacific Ocean

Indian Ocean

Asia

AUSTRALIA

▲ The white sands of the Whitsunday Islands in Queensland form shapes like giant candy meringues. The 74 islands are the peaks of underwater mountain ranges, which were submerged by rising sea levels more than 10,000 years ago.

A Vast Land

Australia is the only country in the world that covers an entire continent. But while Australia is the smallest and least populated of the continents, it is one of the world's largest countries. Australia has many natural resources and much fertile land, but more than a third of the country is desert.

Australian people are not spread evenly throughout their huge country. Most Australians—about 90 percent—live in a few urban areas in the southeast and southwest. These regions generally enjoy more comfortable climates than the rest of Australia. Most of the country's farmland is also located in these areas.

The Outback

The outback contains the country's largest deserts. Large areas of these deserts are very infertile, and little grows in them. It is not possible to grow modern food or other useful crops. Daytime summer temperatures are scorching and there is little water. Travelers have to carry plenty of supplies with them. People have died awaiting rescue when their vehicles have broken down on the isolated roads.

Aboriginal people arrived in Australia about 50,000 years ago. They may have traveled from Asia across

SACRED EARTH

Aboriginal culture is deeply linked with the land, its plants, and its animals. Aboriginal people believe the world was created during the Dreamtime, when their ancestor beings shaped the mountains, rocks, and riverbeds. Wearied by their activity, the ancestors then sank back into the Earth to sleep. Sometimes their spirits became part of the landscape, creating sacred places.

Aboriginal people remember the legends connected to particular places through songs and dances. A song describes a route through the landscape—a songline. At first, the different Aboriginal groups spoke their own languages and had their own art forms and traditions. As the groups came together to share resources, the songlines were extended until they crossed the entire country. Although

▲ The oldest of the Aboriginal paintings in a cave in the Northern Territory are between 18,000 and 20,000 years old. The animals—kangaroos and crocodiles—had spiritual meaning for early Aboriginal hunters.

a songline is invisible, it can be used as a kind of map that lists certain landmarks. Aboriginal people traditionally used them to find their way around.

land bridges that were exposed when sea levels were lower. They have learned to cope with the harsh conditions of the outback. Some still live traditional lifestyles there, although many have moved to towns and cities. Most other residents of the outback are ranchers. They live on stations, huge properties that cover thousands of acres and have thousands of cattle or sheep. Settlements are often very isolated. The outback is one of the world's most important mining regions. Some of the largest mines on Earth are located there—producing metal ores, minerals, and precious stones.

The outback has played an important role in the Australian imagination. There are many tales about early Australians who lived there beyond the reach

THE EMPTY LAKE

Most of the time it is hard to tell that Lake Eyre in South Australia is a lake at all. Its flat salt-encrusted bottom glistens in the sun. The desert region in which the lake lies receives less than 5 inches (12.5 cm) of rain a year, and rivers only empty into the lake when they flood. The rest of the time their water evaporates before it reaches the lake. The lake normally holds a little water every decade or so, but it has been full only three times in the last 150 years. When it is full, waterbirds, such as pelicans, come from miles around. No one knows how the birds realize there is water in the lake. It takes about two years for the lake to dry out again.

▲ This rare view of Lake Eyre filled with water was taken from the air after a flood in 2000.

When the lake is dry, a tiny lizard called the Lake Eyre dragon lives among the cracks in the salt. It has special eyelashes that cut out some of the sun's glare. If the dragon gets too hot, it digs down into moist mud beneath the salt. When the lake floods, the dragon moves to the sandy shore where it digs a burrow.

of the law. They included swagmen who traveled from station to station to find work. A swag was a bundle containing bedding and cooking utensils. Australia's best known song, "Waltzing Matilda" tells the story of a swagman camping at a billabong—a seasonal waterhole that floods only occasionally.

Great Dividing Range

Running around the eastern and southeastern edge of Australia is the Great Dividing Range. The mountain range stretches for nearly 2,300 miles (3,700 km). It got its name because it was thought to divide the fertile coastal plains from the dry interior. Mount Kosciuszko is its highest peak. The range is the source of many of Australia's most important rivers, including the Murray–Darling and Lachlan. The mountain rainfall also seeps into the ground. This water trickles into the Great Artesian Basin and forms the largest area of groundwater (water within the earth that supplies wells and springs) in the world. The groundwater spreads into a huge underground lake beneath a quarter of Australia. This water is too salty for growing crops but can be used to irrigate grasses for farm animals to eat.

Australian Islands

Off the south coast of Australia is the island of Tasmania. It is cooler and damper than the rest of Australia. Only a half million people live there. Many tourists visit Tasmania to see its dramatic coastlines, lakes, rivers, and dense forest.

▼ **Tree ferns frame Russell Falls, the most visited spot in Mt. Field National Park, Tasmania.**

CRAZY NAME, CRAZY PLACE

Western Australia is home to a remarkable geological formation: the Bungle Bungles. Its huge beehive-shaped domes of rock rise up to 1,896 feet (578 m), worn smooth over millions of years by wind and water. Not only the shapes of the rocks are unusual; they are covered in black and orange stripes. The dark bands are formed by layers of soft rock that allow water to seep through. The rock's moist surface encourages algae and lichens to grow, making the rock dark. The orange bands do not let water through. They have no vegetation, but get their color from iron and manganese.

The first Australians traditionally believed the Bungle Bungles were sacred. Few outsiders knew that they even existed until the mid-1980s when the area became Purnululu National Park. In the Kija language of the local indigenous peoples, "purnululu" means "sandstone."

▲ The domed rocks of the Bungle Bungles stretch for miles. The name is believed to come from bundle bundle, a grass that is common to the region.

Visitors follow hiking trails through the rocks, but the best way to get a clear view of the domes and canyons is by helicopter or airplane.

Australia also includes many smaller islands, some of them far out in the ocean. Norfolk Island is one of the most remote at 1,041 miles (1,676 km) northeast of Sydney. The islanders are the descendants of marooned British sailors, who moved there in the mid-1800s.

Macquarie Island, between Tasmania and Antarctica, is the top of a submerged ridge. It is the only place where rocks from the mantle, usually 4 miles (6 km) beneath Earth's surface, are exposed above sea level.

Crocodiles
and
Dingoes

CROCODILES ARE AUSTRALIA'S largest predators. They have a fearsome reputation. They kill or injure several Australians every year. Australians call the saltwater species "salties;" they live on the coast or in river mouths, but sometimes also in freshwater pools. Freshwater species, called "freshies," are smaller. It is difficult to balance the needs of people with the needs of these large reptiles. Salties and freshies do perform an important role in Australia's ecosystem, preventing overpopulation by herbivores (plant eaters). Australia's ecosystem is an unusual one. It developed with very few outside influences, and as a result, many Australian animals are very different from those living elsewhere in the world.

◀ **Salties can be up to 20 feet (6 m) long. They can pull a water buffalo from the bank and drag it underwater until it drowns.**

ANCIENT DIVERSITY

The map opposite shows Australia's main vegetation zones—or what grows where. They range from the dense rain forests of the Queensland coast to the dry deserts of the interior. About 80 percent of Australia's plant species are found nowhere else. The wollemi pine is one of the world's oldest plants, dating back to the time of the dinosaurs. It was discovered only ten years ago by a bushwalker in New South Wales.

▼ The koala bear is not actually a bear. It is related to the kangaroo. Although the koala is not listed as endangered, its population has dropped 90 percent in ten years.

SPECIES AT RISK

Australia is home to more animal families that occur nowhere else than any other country. But since Europeans arrived, around 23 bird species and 22 mammal species have died out. The following are among those animals currently at risk:

- Australasian bittern (bird)
- Australian sea lion
- Bare-rumped sheathtail bat
- Bettong (marsupial)
- Bilby (marsupial)
- Blue petrel (bird)
- Blue-winged parrot
- Bridled nailtail wallaby
- Chatham albatross (bird)
- Coxen's fig parrot
- Dugong (sea mammal)
- Gilbert's potoroo (marsupial)
- Gouldian finch
- Gray nurse shark
- Leadbeater's possum
- Long-footed potoroo (marsupial)
- Lumholtz's tree-kangaroo
- Mount Glorious torrent frog
- Northern hairy-nosed wombat
- Numbat (marsupial)
- Orange-bellied parrot
- Quokka (marsupial)
- Quoll (marsupial)
- Red-tailed phascogal (marsupial)
- Scrubtit (bird)
- Southern cassowary (bird)
- Speartooth shark
- Spotted quail-thrush (bird)
- Western swamp turtle
- White-bellied frog
- Whooping crane
- Yellow-footed rock wallaby

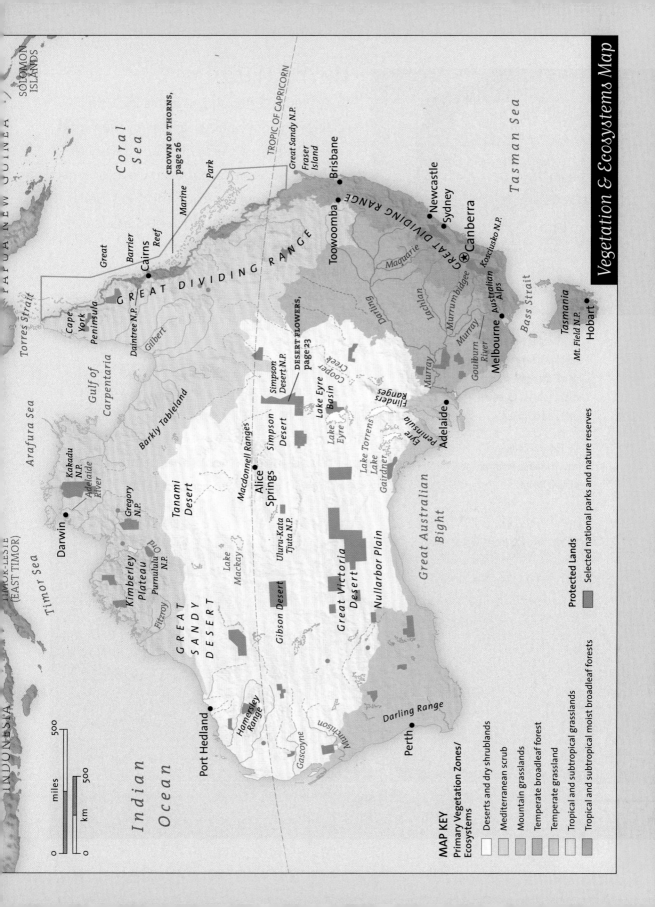

Vegetation & Ecosystems Map

MAP KEY

Primary Vegetation Zones/ Ecosystems

- Deserts and dry shrublands
- Mediterranean scrub
- Mountain grasslands
- Temperate broadleaf forest
- Temperate grassland
- Tropical and subtropical grasslands
- Tropical and subtropical moist broadleaf forests

Protected Lands

- Selected national parks and nature reserves

miles 500

km 500

Indian Ocean

INDONESIA

TIMOR-LESTE (EAST TIMOR)

Timor Sea

Arafura Sea

PAPUA NEW GUINEA

SOLOMON ISLANDS

Coral Sea

Tasman Sea

Gulf of Carpentaria

Torres Strait

Cape York Peninsula

Darwin

Kakadu N.P.

Adelaide River

Gregory N.P.

Kimberley Plateau

Purnululu N.P.

Fitzroy

Port Hedland

Hamersley Range

Gascoyne

Murchison

Darling Range

Perth

Gilbert

Barkly Tableland

Tanami Desert

Lake Mackay

Great Sandy Desert

Gibson Desert

Great Victoria Desert

Nullarbor Plain

Great Australian Bight

Macdonnell Ranges

Alice Springs

Uluru-Kata Tjuta N.P.

Simpson Desert

Simpson Desert N.P.

DESERT FLOWERS, page 23

Lake Eyre Basin

Cooper Creek

Lake Eyre

Lake Eyre

Lake Torrens

Lake Gairdner

Eyre Peninsula

Flinders Ranges

Adelaide

GREAT DIVIDING RANGE

Daintree N.P.

Cairns

Great Barrier Reef

Marine Park

CROWN OF THORNS, page 26

TROPIC OF CAPRICORN

Great Sandy N.P.

Fraser Island

Brisbane

Toowoomba

Newcastle

Sydney

Canberra

Kosciusko N.P.

Australian Alps

Melbourne

Murray

Goulburn River

Murray

Murray

Murrumbidgee

Lachlan

Maquarie

Darling

Bass Strait

Tasmania

Mt. Field N.P.

Hobart

Weird Wildlife

Australia's plants and animals include species from a special group of mammals called marsupials. These mammals give birth to live young that then develop and grow in a pouch on their mother's belly. Nearly half of the world's marsupials live in Australia, including kangaroos, wallabies, wombats, koalas, and Tasmanian devils. A newborn kangaroo has no fur and its eyes are closed. When it is born, it climbs up its mother's fur into her pouch, where it can drink her milk. When it is about six months old, the young kangaroo, or joey, leaves the pouch for short periods. It still hops back in until it grows too large to fit.

Kangaroos are the most widespread of the marsupials. Around 50 different kinds inhabit

▲ The short-nosed echidna has powerful claws for digging and a sticky tongue to catch ants and termites.

▼ The red kangaroo uses its tail to balance when it jumps.

Australia's grasslands living off grasses and leaves. Their huge back legs are remarkably strong. Kangaroos can bound across the ground at about 40 miles per hour (70 km/h). Their tiny front legs are also strong. Some males "box" each other in fights, often in play or for territory.

Australia also contains the world's most ancient living order of mammals and the only egg-laying mammals—the platypus and the echidna.

Forests and Flowers

There are several types of rain forest in Australia. Tropical rain forests, mainly found in northeast Queensland, are the richest in plant and animal species. Subtropical rain forests, close to the mid-eastern coast, contain kauri pine, while cooler broadleaf rain forests are found in parts of the southeast and on Tasmania.

Australia has between 1,200 and 1,400 orchid species, 80 percent of which are not found anywhere else in the world. Many

AUSTRALIA'S "LIVING FOSSIL"

In 1798 a stuffed animal arrived at the British Museum in London from Australia. The specimen had fur, a paddle-like tail, a duck's bill, and webbed feet. It appeared to be a mammal but it was also reported to lay eggs. Scientists thought someone had sewn parts of different animals together as a joke. But it was no joke—it was a platypus. The ancestors of the platypus date back 110 million years to dinosaur days. For this reason, and because some features of its skeleton resemble that of a reptile, the creature is often called a "living fossil."

The platypus lives along waterways in eastern Australia, from Queensland to Tasmania. During the day this shy creature usually rests in a burrow. It hunts for food in the water at night. The platypus is superbly adapted to water. Its coat has two layers: the upper one is so waterproof that the inner layer stays completely dry.

▲ The platypus uses its bill to seek out its food—worms, shrimp, and grubs—that lies hidden on the riverbed. The bill picks up tiny pulses of electricity produced by the nerves and muscles inside prey's bodies.

THE TREE OF LIFE

Eucalyptus trees have dotted the Australian landscape for millions of years. There are more than 600 species of eucalyptus, including the gum tree, mallee, box, ironbark, stringybark, and ash.

Eucalyptus can survive in the poor soils and frequent droughts of the outback. Many of them need forest fires in order to reproduce. The leaves contain oil that fuels fire, and the heat sparks a chemical change that causes new buds to emerge. Hot winds caused by fires also disperse the small seeds by blowing them over long distances.

Eucalyptus are central to entire ecosystems. The koala has evolved to live in eucalyptus trees and it barely eats anything other than eucalyptus leaves. Termites hollow out eucalyptus trunks, turning the wood into a pulp they can eat and build with. The holes they leave form nests for kookaburras, cockatoos, and sugar gliders. Other insects, such as butterflies, feed on eucalyptus leaves and flowers, and in turn are food for birds.

Eucalyptus trees are very important to Australia's economy. Their strong-smelling oil is a powerful natural disinfectant used in medication and perfumes. Because the trees grow quickly, they provide a continuous source of firewood and paper. Many species also provide long, straight wood that can be used for building.

▼ **A fire sweeps across grassland and eucalyptus forest in Queensland.**

species live in tropical forests. Some thrive high up in trees because they do not need nourishment from the soil. Their roots take moisture from the air, and their petals collect rainwater and insects. There are also two species that spend their entire life cycle underground.

In the Australian deserts plants have developed many different ways to survive. The waxy leaves of eucalyptus trees protect them from

the sun and stop them from drying out. Spinifex is a tough grass with spiky leaves that few animals eat, although the plants provide shelter to small animals such as lizards. The scarlet flowers of Sturt's desert pea, named after British explorer Charles Sturt, only appear after a rainfall. The seeds can lie in the ground

▲ Spider orchids are some of the world's most unusually shaped flowers.

▼ Sturt's desert pea flowers in the Simpson Desert, South Australia.

for years without sprouting. When it rains, the flowers last only a few weeks. That is long enough for them to produce seeds, which drop to the ground to wait for the next rain.

Australia's Wild Dog

The dingo, Australia's famous wild dog, is thought to have arrived around 3,500 years ago with Asian seafarers. This mammal is found throughout the Australian mainland,

from the mountains to desert waterholes. Aboriginal peoples used them as hunting dogs and guard dogs. Ranchers consider them pests because they steal livestock—mainly sheep—when other food is scarce.

In the 1800s the world's longest fence was built to keep dingoes out of sheep-farming country in southeastern Australia. The wire-mesh fence stretches 3,307 miles (5,322 km) from Jimbour, near Toowoomba, to the Eyre Peninsula on the southern coast. It was successful at keeping dingoes out, but without dingoes, the rabbit and kangaroo populations increased rapidly, proving the dingo's value in balancing the ecosystem.

▲ Dingoes do not bark, but they have a varied range of howls. They also make a purring sound when contented.

▼ The taipan attacks without warning, biting again and again. Its venom kills in minutes.

Poisonous Critters

Australia is home to many of the deadliest species of animals on the planet. Some live in the deserts, but others live close to people. The majority of deaths in Australia from animal bites and stings are due to allergic reactions to bees and wasps; fatal snakebites occur only a couple of times a year.

However, Australians must be careful. For example, funnel-webs—tiny, black spiders with a deadly bite—are some of the most dangerous spiders in the world. There are 36 species in eastern Australia, where there is enough moisture to keep the spiders cool. They spin funnel-shaped webs around their burrows to trap their prey. Hiding under damp rocks and logs in backyards, they are a risk to unwary gardeners.

Other spiders include the red-back, which spins a small web in dark places, such as among plant pots or under toilet seats. It gives a nasty bite, which hurts a lot but is rarely fatal. The barking spider is not a killer, but it rubs its fangs together to make a scary hiss.

Australia has more than 140 species of snake, of which about 20 are dangerous to humans. They include the tiger snake, the death adder, and a number of sea snakes. The most deadly is the taipan. It produces so much venom that one bite could kill 12,000 guinea pigs.

▼ A funnel-web spider rears up as a tube is used to collect its venom. The poison is used to create antivenom—medicine that stops the effect of venom.

Under Threat

Since the arrival of Europeans over 200 years ago, Australia's wildlife has been badly damaged. The settlers brought animals, such as rats, cats, and rabbits, with them. These creatures began to kill Australian species, or they stole their food and took

THORN IN THE REEF

Australia's Great Barrier Reef is the world's largest area of coral. It sweeps for 1,250 miles (2,012 km) in a crescent along Australia's northeast coast. The reef is made up of about 3,000 separate reef banks, called cays.

Corals are relatives of jellyfish. The reef itself is built up from the shells of dead coral. More than 1,500 fish species, dugongs, and sea lions live among the reefs, and hundreds of bird species live on the coral islands. In 1975 Great Barrier Reef Marine Park was created as one of the world's first national marine sanctuaries.

The corals grow in shallow seas that are at a constant warm temperature. However, global warming could make the water too warm and cause the reef to die. The reef's future is also threatened by a killer starfish. The huge crown-of-thorns starfish eats corals. They clear whole reefs of life. Outbreaks of the starfish are becoming more frequent, but no one knows why. If outbreaks continue, parts of the reef could disappear.

▼ A crown-of-thorns starfish devours a brain coral on the Great Barrier Reef.

over their habitats. As a result, some native species died out and many more are now very rare.

In areas with higher rainfall, farmers cleared the land to make way for fields. At first, Australian farmers used European methods of agriculture. They planted the same types of crops where possible and grazed sheep in other areas. Over the years, this system of farming has turned large areas of Australia into desert. The sheep clear the ground of the thin grass, and the wind blows the soil away before new grass can grow back. Years of watering and then harvesting crops has also damaged the soil in places, making it too salty to grow much at all. Farmers in Australia now manage their water better and sow a mixture of crops that hold the soil together.

Conservation

Australia has 516 national parks covering 3.5 percent of its area. About as much land is classified as protected, helping guard its plants and animals. More protected areas

LIVING ON AND WITH THE LAND

Over thousands of years, Aboriginal people have become experts at surviving in the harsh desert and wet tropical forests of Australia. As they hunted animals and gathered berries, nuts, and plants, they learned to understand the environment. There was often a shortage of food, particularly in central Australia, so Aboriginal people learned to eat things such as lizards, possums, and kangaroos. They dug up witchety grubs, which are caterpillars that live underground. They are highly nutritious. Their food depended on the climate. In more tropical regions they ate fruits and nuts, while coastal tribes hunted for fish. Honey was a popular sweetener, gathered from bees' hives. Traditionally Aboriginal people hunted with spears and heavy, curved throwing sticks. The sticks spun at great speed, killing small animals and stunning larger ones. The boomerang, a smaller, lighter throwing stick, has a sharper curve that brings it back to the thrower if it does not strike its target.

Many Aboriginal groups have animals as their mythical heroes—ancestral spirits who created the land and everything on it. The best known is the Rainbow Serpent, believed to live in waterholes and provide water. Ancient paintings of such animals appear in rock art dating back thousands of years.

▶ **An Aboriginal man shapes a boomerang in the Northern Territory.**

lie off the coast, such as the Great Barrier Reef Marine Park.

Protected areas include Fraser Island, the world's largest sand island; the tropical forest of the Daintree River Valley in Queensland; and the wetlands of Kakadu National Park east of Darwin. The Tasmanian Wilderness World Heritage Area is one of the world's largest wildernesses. It covers a fifth of the island and is home to animals that have died out on the mainland.

Modern Cities, Ancient Land

PEOPLE HAVE LIVED IN AUSTRALIA for 50,000 years—at least 10,000 years longer than in Europe and the Americas. When the first fleet of British settlers arrived in southwestern Australia in January 1788, they lived peacefully with the Aboriginal people. Soon, however, the two groups clashed over who owned the land. This conflict would continue for 200 years.

Many of the new settlers were criminals sent to Australia as a punishment. They were forced to work in harsh conditions, helping to build a settlement around a large harbor. This first town was named Port Jackson, but it later became Sydney, Australia's largest city. Over the years, the port has grown into the home of four million people from 100 different ethnic groups.

◀ **This aerial view of Sydney's Darling Harbour shows the Opera House on the upper left and the Harbour Bridge on the right.**

COLONIZING A CONTINENT

For thousands of years Aborigines lived in Australia. They did not believe that they owned the land, but that they belonged to it. In 1606 European explorers began to visit this huge "new" landmass, which became known as New Holland.

The newcomers brought new ideas of land ownership with them. In 1770, the English explorer James Cook arrived on Australia's east coast. Cook claimed the land in the name of King George III.

▲ A young indigenous boy waits while a group of elders prepare for a corroboree—songs and dances that recall the Dreamtime, a mythical era when spirit beings shaped the world's features.

In 1788 the first settlers arrived. In 1793 free settlers began to arrive in New South Wales. In 1803 Hobart, the capital of Van Diemen's Land (modern Tasmania) was established. Through the 18th and 19th centuries, British settlers started colonies across the continent. In 1901 Australia became a federation of six British colonies.

Time line

This chart shows the approximate dates for the European settlement of Australia; Aboriginal peoples arrived thousands of years earlier.

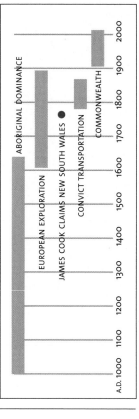

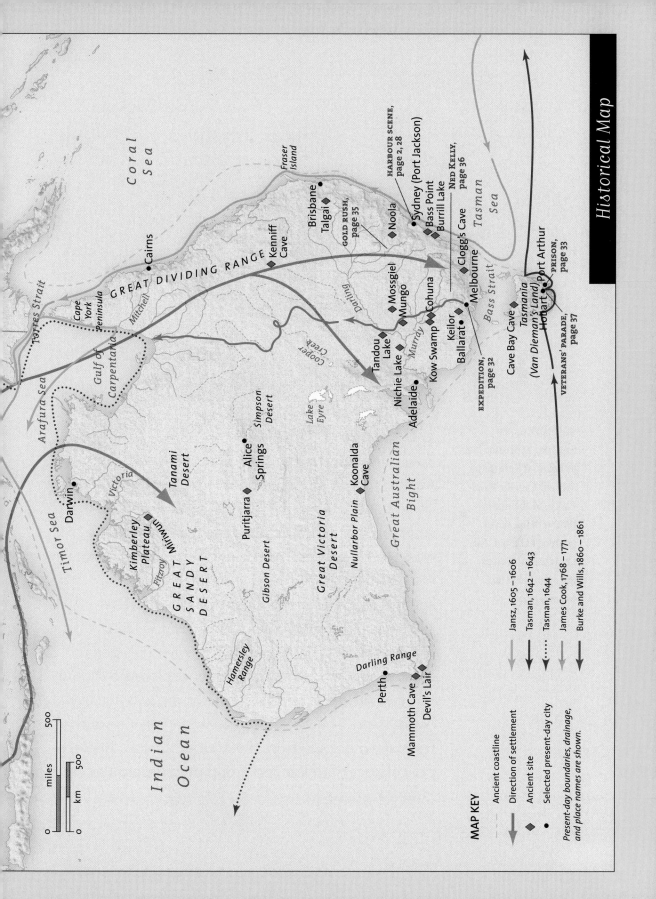

Historical Map

Coral Sea

Fraser Island

Cairns

GREAT DIVIDING RANGE

Kenniff Cave

Brisbane
Talgai

GOLD RUSH, page 35

Noola

HARBOUR SCENE, page 2, 28

Sydney (Port Jackson)

Bass Point
Burrill Lake

NED KELLY, page 36

Mossgiel

Mungo

Cohuna

Clogg's Cave

Melbourne

Tasman Sea

Bass Strait

Kow Swamp

Keilor

Ballarat

Tandou Lake

Murray

Darling

Nichie Lake

EXPEDITION, page 32

Adelaide

Cave Bay Cave

Tasmania
(Van Dieman's Land)

Hobart

Port Arthur

PRISON, page 33

VETERANS' PARADE, page 37

Cooper Creek

Mitchell

Cape York Peninsula

Gulf of Carpentaria

Torres Strait

Arafura Sea

Koonalda Cave

Nullarbor Plain

Great Australian Bight

Lake Eyre

Simpson Desert

Alice Springs

Tanami Desert

Puritjarra

Gibson Desert

Great Victoria Desert

Victoria

Darwin

Timor Sea

Kimberley Plateau

Millnuun

Fitzroy

GREAT SANDY DESERT

Hamersley Range

Indian Ocean

Darling Range

Perth

Mammoth Cave
Devil's Lair

MAP KEY

- - - - Ancient coastline

→ Direction of settlement

◆ Ancient site

● Selected present-day city

Present-day boundaries, drainage, and place names are shown.

Jansz, 1605–1606

Tasman, 1642–1643

Tasman, 1644

James Cook, 1768–1771

Burke and Wills, 1860–1861

miles 0 — 500

km 0 — 500

Unknown Interior

Four hundred years ago, no Europeans had seen Australia. Even so, some people believed that a great continent existed in the Southern Hemisphere—the southern half of the globe. They thought that the world was balanced. Because there were continents in the Northern Hemisphere, they must also exist in the south. The unknown continent was called *Terra Australis*, or "southern land." In 1606 the Dutch explorer William Jansz became the first European to see the new land. It took years for explorers to figure out that Australia, as it became known, was actually a huge island. The interior remained largely unexplored for many more years. In 1860 Robert O'Hara Burke, a police officer, led the first group of Europeans to cross

Australia. The expedition traveled from the south to the north coast, but on the way back all but one of the explorers died of exhaustion and starvation.

A Dumping Ground

The British were one of the first European peoples to claim Australia after James Cook explored the coast in 1770. In Britain the prisons were overcrowded. The government decided the new land was the ideal place to send its convicts. In 1788 a fleet of 11 ships brought 588 male and 188 female convicts to Port Jackson. Soon afterward prison colonies were set up in New South Wales, Norfolk Island, and Van Diemen's Land. Australia became a dumping ground.

A PLACE OF MISERY

The isolated prison at Port Arthur on the Tasman Peninsula in Van Diemen's Land (modern Tasmania) was built as a place of punishment for the worst criminals. Hard labor included stone cutting, construction, and coal-mining. Punishment cells were small, pitch dark, and contained nothing but a dirty rug to lie on.

There was a special prison for boys between nine and 18 years old. Their day was spent in general labor, classes in practical trades like bootmaking, and prayer.

Escape from Port Arthur was almost impossible, as shark-infested waters surrounded three sides of the prison while the landward side was heavily guarded. Some men found life there so hard that they committed murder just so they would be punished by death.

▲ The ruins of the huge penitentiary at Port Arthur, which was known as "Hell on Earth."

Unlike the Aboriginal people, the new arrivals (convicts and settlers alike) had little idea what plants or animals they could eat or how to find them. They nearly starved to death. Convicts continued to be sent to Australia for another 80 years. Most had been convicted of minor crimes, such as theft, but their sentences were harsh. Those who managed to escape from the penal colonies usually died in the outback.

Growing Population

Over the next hundred years, more free immigrants arrived. As the population grew and settlements emerged, the country began to be economically successful. In the 1800s sheep farming expanded rapidly. Britain had new factories to produce wool. Australia had lots of pasture land to raise sheep to supply them.

▼ Sheep stations, like this one in Queensland, can have as many as 100,000 sheep.

AUSTRALIA'S GOLD RUSH

In 1851 gold was found in Victoria. The discovery started the world's richest gold rush. Within two months there were a thousand miners in the new town of Ballarat, near Melbourne. By 1853 the town had more than 20,000 immigrants from all over Australia and the world. Over the next four years, millions of ounces of gold were transported under police escort to the Melbourne Treasury, while more was sold secretly and illegally. Before long, the alluvial (river and stream) deposits of surface gold began to dwindle, and hundreds of companies were formed to dig deeper underground. Other industries grew to meet the needs of the miners. The gold rush not only brought great wealth to individuals; it also had a very large and lasting effect on the development of the nation.

▲ Prospectors pan for gold near the Turon River in New South Wales. In the early days of the Turon gold rush, miners could collect as much as four ounces of gold from sifting 10 buckets of river dirt.

In the middle of the 1800s, Australia got a new reputation, as a source of gold. In 1851 a gold rush began in Victoria and New South Wales. Australia's population more than doubled in just 10 years. The immigrants did not all find gold, but there were plenty of other minerals, such as copper, tin, and silver. New railroads, roads, and irrigation systems were built to meet the needs of the new settlers.

By 1859 six colonies existed, each with its own government: New South Wales, Tasmania, Western Australia, South Australia, Victoria, and Queensland. In 1901 the colonies joined to form a commonwealth of the British Empire with a central government with

HERO OR VILLAIN?

One of Australia's most famous folk heroes is outlaw Edward "Ned" Kelly. He was born in 1855 to a father who had been transported from Ireland to the penal colony on Van Diemen's Land for stealing pigs. Ned's early teenage years were spent breaking-in horses and rounding up cattle. But times were hard, and he soon turned to horse stealing and cattle rustling.

Ned's family was often in trouble with the police. Ned and his brother, Dan, became outlaws. Two friends joined them on the run. The Kelly Gang robbed two banks and killed three police officers and a witness to their crimes. After a chase, the police cornered the gang. In the shoot-out, three of the gang were killed. Ned Kelly was wearing armor he had made from pieces of an iron plow. When he emerged from his hideout, however, bullets tore into his arms and legs and he was captured. Ned was tried and hanged in Melbourne in 1880, despite public petitions for mercy. Today many Australians are still torn about how they see Ned Kelly. On one hand, he was a criminal and a killer; but on the other hand, many people have a quiet regard for him as a hero who shared Australians' traditional rebellious attitude towards authority.

▲ This print from 1880 shows Ned Kelly in the suit of armor he made from old plow parts. It weighed 90 pounds (40 kg).

limited powers. The Australian Capital Territory (ACT) and the Northern Territory later joined the federation.

International Power

In the 20th century, Australia played an important role in world affairs. It joined Britain in fighting World War I (1914–1918). Each April 25, Australians remember the Australian and New Zealand Army

Corps (Anzacs). Anzac Day marks a 1915 landing on the Gallipoli Peninsula in Turkey, one of the enemy powers. The troops landed in the wrong place and were trapped on the beaches. The Anzacs fought bravely for months and became a symbol of Australians' courage and independent spirit.

Australian troops went on to fight in World War II (1939–1945), the Korean War in the 1950s, and the Vietnam War in the 1960s and 1970s. Later, Australia took part in peace-keeping actions for the United Nations, mainly in Asia. By the start of the 21st century, it had confirmed its position as a major power in the region.

▲ Veterans proudly display their medals as they march in an Anzac Day parade in Hobart, Tasmania.

Good Sports

ADELAIDE WRITERS' WEEK is one of the largest literary festivals anywhere. Visitors hear authors from all over the world read and discuss their work. The city also hosts a Festival of Arts, a Festival of Ideas, and the Adelaide Fringe, which presents theater shows. Australia's image was traditionally that of a rough-and-ready country, better known for its sports than for its culture. That reputation was shaped by the tough conditions facing the early settlers and Australia's position far from cultural centers in Europe and America. Although Australians still pride themselves on being down to earth, today they are also likely to be creative. Each state has its own arts festival, and Australian writers, artists, and filmmakers are celebrated at home and around the world.

◀ **A brightly costumed girl takes some time out at Adelaide's Come Out Festival, which is aimed at school children of all ages.**

WHO IS AN AUSTRALIAN?

Nearly a quarter of the Australian population was born outside the country but has moved to live there. They come from United Kingdom and Italy, but also from China, Vietnam, North Africa, and the Middle East. The newcomers make Australia one of the world's most ethnically varied nations, with a wide range of religions, foods, and languages. So just who is an Australian? Around a third of the population claim "Australian" ancestry. They include Aboriginal peoples, but also people descended from earlier European settlers. Some people believe that new arrivals become Australians simply by choosing to live in the country; others argue that only people born in Australia are Australians.

1950 / 8 million	1970 / 13 million
25% Rural · 75% Urban	15% Rural · 85% Urban

1990 / 17 million	2005 / 20 million
15% Rural · 85% Urban	7% Rural · 93% Urban

Common Australian Phrases

Australians use many of the same everyday phrases and greetings as Americans and Britons, but with local variations. Here are a few words you might hear in Australia:

Arvo	afternoon
Aussie	an Australian
Billabong	a pool of water left in a dry river bed
Bonza	great
Chook	chicken
Crook	unwell
Fair dinkum	someone or something genuine
G'day	hello
No worries	no problem at all
Tucker	food
Ute	utility vehicle or pickup truck

▶ The outback town of Oodnadatta has a population of about 230 and consists of one main street.

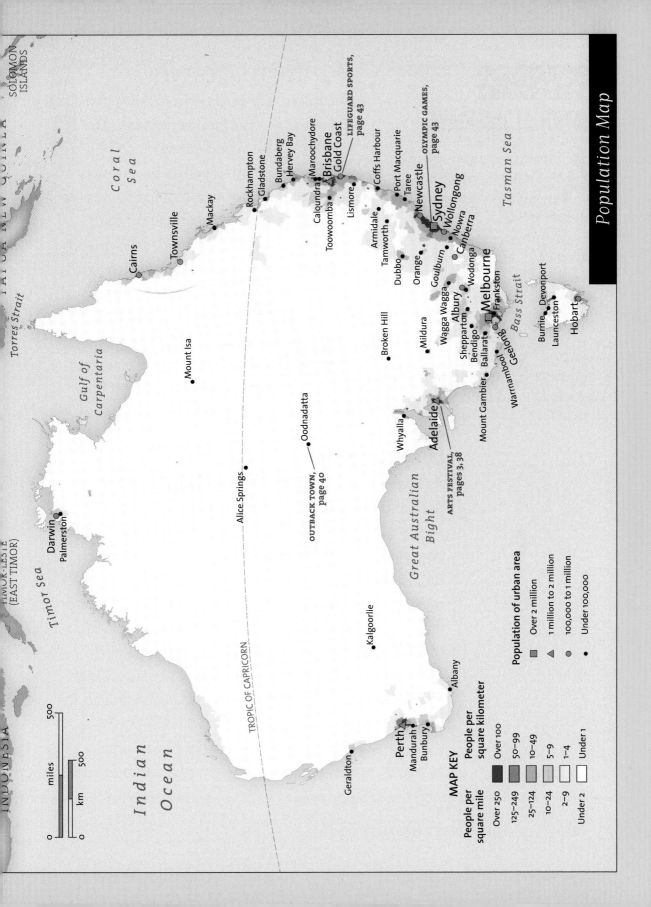

Population Map

SOLOMON ISLANDS

Coral Sea

Cairns
Townsville
Mackay
Rockhampton
Gladstone
Bundaberg
Hervey Bay
Maroochydore
Caloundra
Brisbane
Gold Coast
LIFEGUARD SPORTS, page 43
Toowoomba
Lismore
Coffs Harbour
Armidale
Tamworth
Port Macquarie
Taree
Newcastle
Sydney
Wollongong
OLYMPIC GAMES, page 43
Nowra
Canberra
Dubbo
Orange
Goulburn
Wodonga
Albury
Wagga Wagga
Mildura
Shepparton
Bendigo
Ballarat
Melbourne
Frankston
Geelong
Warrnambool
Mount Gambier
Burnie
Devonport
Launceston
Hobart

Tasman Sea

Bass Strait

Broken Hill
Whyalla
Adelaide
ARTS FESTIVAL, pages 3, 38

Great Australian Bight

Oodnadatta
OUTBACK TOWN, page 40

Mount Isa

Gulf of Carpentaria

Alice Springs

Torres Strait

PAPUA NEW GUINEA

Darwin
Palmerston

Timor Sea

TIMOR-LESTE (EAST TIMOR)

INDONESIA

Kalgoorlie

Geraldton
Perth
Mandurah
Bunbury
Albany

TROPIC OF CAPRICORN

Indian Ocean

MAP KEY

People per square mile

	People per square kilometer
Over 250	Over 100
125–249	50–99
25–124	10–49
10–24	5–9
2–9	1–4
Under 2	Under 1

Population of urban area

- ■ Over 2 million
- ▲ 1 million to 2 million
- ● 100,000 to 1 million
- • Under 100,000

miles 500

km 500

0

Outdoor Lifestyle

Australia's way of life ensures that people are outdoors as often as possible. The weather is warm and sunny much of the year, and even major cities have plenty of parks for relaxing. In the outback, people go bushwalking or touring in off-road vehicles. Swimming, surfing, sailing, and fishing are all popular at the beach. Many families spend the day there, sharing picnics with their friends. City and suburban families regularly dine in restaurants and cafes, but barbecuing at home is also popular—even Christmas lunch is sometimes cooked this way.

G'Day Sport!

Australians love sports. Although tennis, swimming, golf, and horse racing are popular, more people enjoy sports such as cricket, soccer, and rugby. Their popularity reflects Australia's close connections with Britain where they were originally invented. Australia's most watched sport is a ball game that they invented themselves. Australian rules football is a combination of Gaelic football and an Aboriginal sport named *marn grook*. It is seldom played elsewhere. In winter, snowboarding and skiing draw many Australians to the eastern mountain slopes.

Australia also has a proud history of competing at the Olympics. It is one of only three countries that

CATHY FREEMAN

It was a hugely symbolic moment when Cathy Freeman lit the Olympic flame at the Sydney Games in 2000. Freeman was an Aboriginal athlete representing her home country. With a whole nation watching, Freeman went on to win the women's 400 meters. She was the first Aboriginal person to win an individual Olympic gold medal.

Freeman had become well known in the 1990s. As she began to win races, she celebrated by running victory laps draped in both the Australian and the Aboriginal flags. In 1997 she became the 400-meter world champion, which helped her win the prestigious Australian of the Year award the following year. Freeman's success has received so much attention because Aboriginal athletes are not common in international sports.

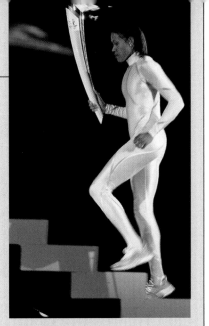

▲ Cathy Freeman at the opening ceremony of the Olympic Games

has competed at every modern Olympic Games. The games have been staged in Australia twice, in Sydney (2000) and Melbourne (1956).

Music from the Roots

Aboriginal culture has a powerful influence in Australia. Traditional artists paint "x-ray" images on tree bark.

▼ Lifeguards charge for the water at the start of a surfing competition on the Gold Coast in Queensland.

DAME NELLIE MELBA

One hundred years ago, Nellie Melba was Australia's first singing superstar. Born Helen Porter Mitchell in Melbourne in 1861, she learned singing at a young age. Her father took her to Europe, where she studied in Paris with a celebrated teacher. She made up the stage name Nellie Melba using her hometown as inspiration. In 1887 Melba made her operatic debut in Brussels, Belgium. She went on to sing in London, Paris, Milan, and New York. Melba was popular wherever she went, becoming renowned for the purity and range of her voice. For many people she was a symbol of a highly polished and sensitive side of the Australian character.

Melba returned to Australia in 1902 but continued to travel, performing widely. In 1918 the Queen made her a dame (the female equivalent of a knight). In 1920 Melba was the first international artist to make a live radio broadcast. She died in 1931. Melba toast and peach melba dessert are named after her.

▼ **The didgeridoo is an ancient instrument. They were depicted in rock paintings at least 1,500 years ago.**

These pictures show animals' bones and organs. Musicians still play traditional instruments such as the didgeridoo, which makes a droning sound. The instrument is made from a eucalyptus branch hollowed out by termites. Aboriginal music is still changing: The band Yothu Yindi mixes traditional music with modern rock.

Living in the Outback

Life in the outback is a big contrast to city life. Many services are not available. The few schools, hospitals, and doctors are far apart. Children study over the radio with the School of the Air and medical treatment comes from the Royal Flying Doctor Service

(RFDS). RFDS doctors hold clinics in isolated areas and carry out consultations by radio. In an emergency, patients are airlifted to the hospital. Airplanes land on flat airstrips, or even on a highway.

In the outback, most food comes from the farm, and a diesel generator produces electricity. The mail arrives once a month, and often there is no TV reception. But the government is investing to improve communications. Soon better radio and high-speed Internet connections may bring the outback in closer touch with the rest of Australia.

SCHOOL WITHOUT CLASSES

Children in the remote outback cannot travel to schools, which are usually too far away. Instead, School of the Air comes to them. Its teachers used to give lessons over the radio using a shortwave receiver. Children sent in their assignments via the flying doctor or the mail. Since 2002, many children have switched to Internet lessons. Students with broadband connections can watch their teachers live on a video feed and talk with them through their computers.

Most teachers are based at major towns such as Alice Springs or Broken Hill. Sometimes children have one-on-one lessons, at other times a "class" of children all follow the same lesson—but classmates may never meet each other. Lessons tend to last for about an hour in the morning. Then students concentrate on their projects, usually with supervision from a parent or tutor. Now students can send in their work by e-mail and get their grades the same way.

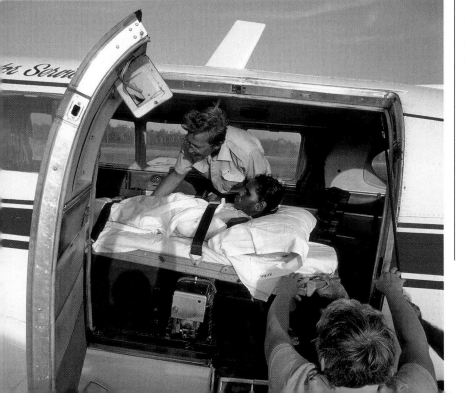

◀ A patient is loaded onto an airplane operated by the Royal Flying Doctor Service.

Creating *a* Nation

WHEN AUSTRALIA'S SIX COLONIES formed a federation, or union, in 1901, there was a heated debate about whether Sydney or Melbourne should be the capital. It took ten years to reach a compromise. Melbourne was to remain the country's capital while a new one was created. New South Wales gave land to the government for that purpose. It became the Australian Capital Territory (ACT) in 1938. The city of Canberra was built around Lake Burley Griffin, a large artificial lake named after the U.S. architect who had won the competition to design the new city. In 1927 the Provisional Parliament House opened, and Canberra officially became the seat of the federal government. The ACT became a self-governing territory in 1989.

◀ The new Parliament House in Canberra has been in use since 1988. The building's huge courtyard is decorated with a mosaic of an Aboriginal artwork.

SHARING POWER

Australia has six states and two territories. When Australia became a Commonwealth in 1901, powers were shared between the national government—the Commonwealth—and the six states. The Constitution sets out the legislative (lawmaking) powers of the Commonwealth and of the states and territories. These rules cannot be changed, except by public vote. The federal government is allowed to change or even abolish the legislative powers of the two territories—the Australian Capital Territory (ACT) and Northern Territory. It also administers Ashmore and Cartier, Christmas, Cocos (or Keeling), Coral Sea, Heard, McDonald, and Norfolk islands and Jervis Bay. The political map opposite shows Australia's states and territories, and their capital cities.

▼ **Prime Minister John Howard announces his cabinet after winning a fourth consecutive term in 2004.**

Trading Partners

Australia has a strong economy, helped by its growing links with China. Its chief exports include coal, gold, meat, and wool, while its main imports include machinery and transportation equipment, computers, office machines, telecommunications equipment, and crude oil.

Country	Percent Australia exports
Japan	20.3%
China	11.5%
South Korea	7.9%
United States	6.7%
All others combined	53.6%

Country	Percent Australia imports
United States	13.9%
China	13.7%
Japan	11.0%
Singapore	5.6%
All others combined	55.8%

Political Map

Political Parties and Elections

Three parties dominate politics: the Liberal Party, the National Party, and the Australian Labour Party (ALP). The Liberals and Nationals shared power in 1996 when John Howard became prime minister.

Australians believe that citizenship is not just a right but a responsibility. Citizens have to play a part in the government of the country, so everyone over the age of 18 has to vote. Anyone who does not show up at the poll on election day is fined unless they prove that they had a good reason. To help people get to the polls, elections are held on Saturdays and people can vote anywhere in their state. Voters in remote areas cast their ballots earlier or by mail.

HOW THE GOVERNMENT WORKS

The British Queen is Australia's chief of state. She appoints a governor-general to represent her in parliament. The governor-general swears in the prime minister, who is the leader of the party that wins most seats in a general election. The prime minister nominates members of parliament to form the cabinet. The governor-general appoints the chief justice and six other justices to the High Court. Half of the Senate state members are elected every three years to serve six-year terms while all territory members are elected every three years. House of Representatives members are elected for terms of up to three years.

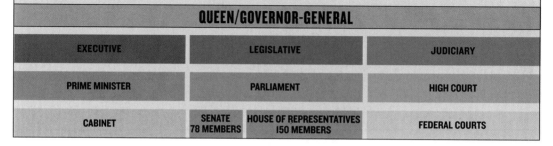

QUEEN/GOVERNOR-GENERAL		
EXECUTIVE	LEGISLATIVE	JUDICIARY
PRIME MINISTER	PARLIAMENT	HIGH COURT
CABINET	SENATE 78 MEMBERS · HOUSE OF REPRESENTATIVES 150 MEMBERS	FEDERAL COURTS

Becoming a Republic

Australia's head of state is the British monarch, who is represented in Australia by the governor-general. Many Australians think that the arrangement reflects the past and that the country should have its own head of state. They want Australia to become a republic headed by an elected president. Others believe that the monarchy brings stability; they see no reason to make changes.

▼ The Queen greets onlookers at the Aquatic Centre in Melbourne during the 2006 Commonwealth Games.

Australians have been arguing about the issue for over a century. In 1999 the government held a vote to give Australians a chance to decide. Voters decided against a republic—but not by a big enough margin to end the debate.

Traditional Earners

Australia is an important exporter of agricultural products. Agriculture used to earn almost 80 percent

▼ "No" supporters add a banner above the "Yes" banner outside a polling booth during the 1999 referendum.

SHEEP STATIONS

Sheep came to Australia with the first European settlers. They were kept for their meat but soon they were also bred for their wool. The animals flourished, particularly after the introduction of the merino breed in 1797. For all of its history since that date, Australia has had more sheep than people. Today there are 120 million sheep—and only 20 million Australians. About three-quarters of the sheep are merinos. They produce wool that is one of Australia's main exports.

The animals are raised on vast ranches called sheep stations. A station might be thousands of square miles in area. It has to be big because grass grows only thinly on dry land, and the flock must keep moving to find all the food it needs. At regular periods the sheep have to be rounded up. They are dipped in chemicals to protect them from fleas and other bugs or sheared of their thick wool before the summer. Farmhands round the sheep up on horseback or on motorbike, helped by trained sheepdogs. Teams of professional shearers travel around the stations. They work nine-hour days as they shear herds of 4,000 or more sheep at a time.

▲ A sheep shearer in action on a Tasmanian sheep station. The fleece is removed in one piece using a tool like an electric razor. A good shearer can fleece around 200 sheep a day.

A professional shearer can remove a fleece in less than two minutes.

Sheep farming is a risky business. Farmers need rain for the grass to grow, and low wool prices will also wipe out their profits. Many of them grow crops, such as wheat, to bring in extra money. They must work hard, and life is also challenging for their families. Many farm children go away to boarding school.

of Australia's income from exports (things sold abroad). Wool and wheat are still the most important products, followed by meat (particularly beef), sugar, cotton, dairy products, wine, and fruit. Since the 1950s, however, the economy has broadened to include more nonagricultural areas.

Another major industry is mining. Australia had major gold rushes in the 1850s and 1890s. Today's industry is much more professional and heavily controlled: about 300 tons of gold a year makes Australia the fourth largest gold producer in the world. The discovery of other minerals in the 1950s and 1960s—oil, gas, iron ore, bauxite, and coal—means

▲ Tugs bring an oil tanker into Sydney Harbour. The ship has just passed Bennelong Point, the site of one of the most distinctive 20th-century buildings in the world— the Sydney Opera House.

that mineral and energy exports now provide more than 35 percent of Australia's export earnings.

Many mines are in remote regions. Mining companies fly skilled workers in, often from thousands of miles away. The miners live in housing next to the mine, and they often fly back home for vacations. Fly In, Fly Out (FIFO) is a way of life for half of Western Australia's mine workers.

INDUSTRY

This map shows the locations of some of Australia's main industrial and mining operations. At first factories made goods for sale in Australia, but the country soon began to sell products abroad. That reached a peak in the 1960s. Since then many companies have moved their factories to Asia where labor is cheaper. Far fewer Australians now work in manufacturing industries.

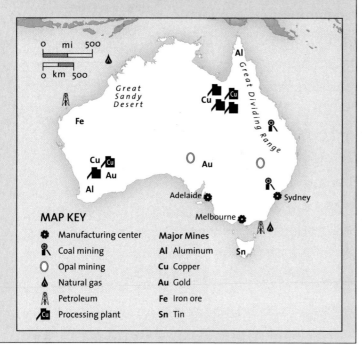

MAP KEY

- Manufacturing center
- Coal mining
- Opal mining
- Natural gas
- Petroleum
- Processing plant

Major Mines
- **Al** Aluminum
- **Cu** Copper
- **Au** Gold
- **Fe** Iron ore
- **Sn** Tin

New Partners

Traditionally Australia looked toward Great Britain as its chief trading partner. However, recently Australia has looked for business closer to home. In 1989 Australia helped start the Asia-Pacific Economic Cooperation (APEC), a group of 21 countries from around the Pacific Ocean, including Japan, China, the United States, and Russia. APEC aims to make it easier for the Pacific countries to trade with one another. Australia has also signed its own trade agreements

MINERS WHO LIVE UNDERGROUND

Imagine a town where you and your neighbors live underground. At Coober Pedy in South Australia that's how 80 percent of the population live. Below ground is the coolest place to be. Outside, the summer temperatures reach over 122° F (50° C). Underground, the rocky rooms stay cool in summer—but also do not get too cold on winter nights. Although homes and shops are carved into the rock, they are not like caves. They are tiled and neat; some are quite luxurious.

Precious stones bring people from more than 45 countries to this unusual town. Opals were discovered there in 1915 by Willie Hutchinson. The first miners to live underground were said to have been veterans of World War I who were used to living in trenches and underground barracks. The town's unusual name came from the Aboriginal phrase "kupa piti," which means something like "white man in a hole." The town became known as the "opal capital of the world."

▲ Coober Pedy's underground church always remains cool in the desert heat.

with China, New Zealand, Thailand, Papua New Guinea, Singapore, and the United States.

One result of improving trade is that the economy has grown steadily since 1990. Australia was the world's 17th-wealthiest nation in 2005. So few Australians were unemployed that observers began to worry that the country would face a labor and skills shortage.

▼ The Super Pit at Kalgoorlie is Australia's largest open-cut gold mine. It is worked 24 hours a day every day of the year.

A Trip Down Under

About six percent of Australians work in tourism, which is one of the country's most important industries. Many visitors are attracted by the miles of coastline, the daily sunshine, and the lively cities. Others come to experience Australia's unique wildlife, or the traditional culture of the Aborigines.

The tourists come mainly from New Zealand, Europe, the United States, and Japan. Many are young backpackers who want to experience Australian culture. They often take seasonal jobs such as harvesting grapes in the vineyards.

▼ A saltwater crocodile thrills tourists on the Adelaide River as food is thrown off the boat.

▼ Tourists pretend to push over one of the Devil's Marbles, a rock formation near Alice Springs.

A New Century

Australians began the 21st century well. The Olympic Games in Sydney in 2000 raised Australia's profile in the world. But the new century also poses challenges. The average age of Australians is getting higher. Soon the country will need many more younger workers. Traditionally, Australia has welcomed immigrants from many parts of the world, especially from Europe, Asia, and the Pacific Islands. That mix of people has helped make Australia a successful country.

With its high standards of living, Australia is still a favorite place to move, and there is no shortage of people wanting to come. Since the average age of Australians is getting higher and people are retiring from their jobs, the steady flow of immigrants is beneficial. Immigrants join the workforce, which balances out the country's need for younger workers. At the same time, a strong workforce helps grow the nation's economy. Australia has come a long way since its days as a prison colony, and with an educated population and strong financial system, its future looks very bright.

▼ Darling Harbour, in the center of Sydney, has recently been redeveloped, helping to make the city a world center of business, art, and entertainment.

Add a Little Extra to Your Country Report!

I f you are assigned to write a report about Australia, you'll want to include basic information about the country, of course. The Fast Facts chart on page 8 will give you a good start. The rest of the book will give you the details you need to create a full and up-to-date paper or PowerPoint presentation. But what can you do to make your report more fun than anyone else's? If you use your imagination and dig a bit deeper into some of the topics introduced in this book, you're sure to come up with information that will make your report unique!

>Flag

Perhaps you could explain the history of Australia's flag, and the meanings of its colors and symbols. Go to **www.crwflags.com/fotw/flags** for more information.

>National Anthem

How about downloading Australia's national anthem, and playing it for your class? At **www.nationalanthems.info** you'll find what you need, including the words to the anthem, plus sheet music for the anthem. Simply pick "A" and then "Australia" from the list on the left-hand side of the screen, and you're on your way.

>Time Difference

If you want to understand the time difference between Australia and where you are, this Web site can help: **www.worldtimeserver.com**. Just pick "Australia" from the list on the left. If you called Australia right now, would you wake whomever you are calling from their sleep?

>Currency

Another Web site will convert your money into dollars, the currency used in Australia. You'll want to know how much money to bring if you're ever lucky enough to travel to Australia: **www.xe.com/ucc**.

>Weather

Why not check the current weather in Australia? It's easy—simply go to **www.weather.com** to find out if it's sunny or cloudy, warm or cold in Australia right this minute! Pick "World" from the headings at the top of the page. Then search for Australia. Click on any city you like. Be sure to click on the tabs below the weather report for Sunrise/Sunset information, Weather Watch, and Business Travel Outlook, too. Scroll down the page for the 36-hour Forecast and a satellite weather map. Compare your weather to the weather in the Australian city you chose. Is this a good season, weather-wise, for a person to travel to Australia?

>Miscellaneous

Still want more information? Simply go to National Geographic's One-Stop Research site at **http://www.nationalgeographic.com/onestop**. It will help you find maps, photos and art, articles and information, games and features that you can use to jazz up your report.

Glossary

Antivenom a medicine made from an animal's venom that is used to reverse the effects of a venomous bite.

Bushwalker a hiker in a wooded or remote area.

Cabinet a group of politicians who run a country. Each member of the cabinet is in charge of a particular part of the government.

Carcass the remains of a dead body.

Carnivore a meat-eating animal.

Colony generally, a region ruled by a nation located somewhere else in the world. In Australia, a political unit with its own form of government, which in 1901 became a state within the new federation.

Commonwealth a nation or state governed by the people.

Convict a criminal who has been found guilty and sent to prison.

Coral reef A large underwater structure made from the skeletons of many tiny jelly-like animals called coral polyps.

Culture a collection of beliefs, traditions, and styles that belong to people living in a certain part of the world.

Desert an extremely dry area, where yearly precipitation (hail, rain, and snow) is less than 10 inches (25 mm).

Ethnic group a large section of a country's population with members that share a common ancestry or background.

Federation a group of small states that gather together to form a larger country.

Fertile when land is good for growing plants.

Fossil the remains of a plant or animal that lived millions of years ago and has been preserved in some way.

Gold rush when many miners and adventurers head for the same location to try to find large amounts of gold.

Habitat a part of the environment that is suitable for certain plants and animals.

Hemisphere one half of a sphere, or globe. The Earth is generally divided into the Northern and Southern Hemisphere. Australia is in the Southern Hemisphere.

Native a person or species that is originally from a certain country.

Order a large group of closely related animals.

Peace-keeping mission when a military force is sent into trouble spots and war zones to prevent violence.

Penal colony a prison that is based abroad.

Peninsula a narrow piece of land that is surrounded by water on three sides. The word means "almost island" in Latin.

Species a type of organism; animals or plants in the same species look similar and can only breed successfully among themselves.

Swagman an Australian drifter, who carried his belongings, or swag, with him.

Urban an area that has many buildings and is crowded with people.

Venom a poison injected by an animal into the body of its prey or predators.

Veteran a soldier who has fought in a war.

Bibliography

Alter, J. *Discovering Australia's Land, People, and Wildlife.* Berkeley Heights, NJ: My-ReportLinks.com Books, 2004.

Kerns, Ann. *Australia in Pictures.* Minneapolis: Lerner Publications Co., 2004.

http://www.asknow.gov.au
(Australian reference librarians answer your questions)

http://www.csu.edu.au/australia/
(general information)

http://www.cultureand recreation.gov.au/articles/australianhistory/
(history of the European settlement of Australia)

http://www.dreamtime.net.au/
(information on Australia's indigenous people)

Further Information

NATIONAL GEOGRAPHIC Articles

Daly, Margo. "Eat, Drink, Art, Sydney." NATIONAL GEOGRAPHIC TRAVELER (May/June 2006): 36.

Gordon, David George. "Go On Safari! Destination: Australia." NATIONAL GEOGRAPHIC KIDS (September 2006): 44-45.

Web sites to explore

More fast facts about Australia, from the CIA (Central Intelligence Agency): https://www.cia.gov/cia/publications/factbook/geos/as.html

Thinking of being one of the many tourists that visits Australia each year? The country's official tourism site has all you need to know: http://www.australia.com

Do you want to know more about Australia's fascinating wildlife? This site has plenty of information about marsupials, dingoes, and other interesting animals: http://www.aussie-info.com/identity/fauna/index.php

What's it like in the outback? Find out with this site: http://www.wilderness.org.au/campaigns/outback/

See, hear

There are many ways to get a taste of life in Australia, including movies, music CDs, and TV shows. You might be able to locate these:

Walkabout (1971) ·
A movie about three children lost in the outback and how the experience changes them.

Rabbit-proof Fence (2002)
This movie is the story of three indigenous girls taken from their parents to be trained as household servants.

Gallipoli (1981)
Mel Gibson is the star of this movie about Australians fighting in World War I.

The Dish (2000)
This comedy tells how an Australian radio telescope played a vital part in the Apollo moonlanding of 1969.

Tribal Voice (2006)
This CD is by Yothu Yindi, a band famous for mixing indigenous and rock music.

Heartbreak High
This soap opera about a Sydney high school was an international hit for six years; you may be able to find it on the Internet.

Index

Credits

Picture Credits

Front Cover – Spine: Rafael Joan Gomez Pons/Shutterstock; Top: Annie Griffiths Belt/NGIC; Low far left: Jason Edwards/NGIC; Low left: Medford Taylor/NGIC; Low right: Penny Tweedie/Corbis; Low far right: Steve Bowman/Corbis.

Interior – Corbis: 32 up, 35 up, 36 up; Bettmann: 44 up; Robert Essel NYC: TP; David Grey/Reuters: 55 lo; Kit Kittle: 45 lo; POOL/Reuters: 51 up; Reuters: 25 center, 43 up, 51 lo; Paul A. Souders: 3 left, 38-39; Graham Taylor/Canberra Times: 48 lo; Penny Tweedie: 3 right, 46-47; Patrick Ward: 53 up; NG Image Collection: Sam Abell: 14 lo, 22 lo; Jonathan Blair: 23 up; Paul Chesley: 10 up, 30 lo; David Doubilet: 26 lo; Nicole Duplaix 15 up, 21 lo, 24 lo; Jason Edwards: 13 up, 24 up, 33 lo, 40 up, 55 up; Annie Griffiths Belt: 2-3, 28-29, 57 center; R. Ian Lloyd: 43 lo; Gerd Ludwig: 37 up, 52 up; Richard Nowitz: 27 center, 44 lo; Randy Olson: 2 right, 16-17, 56 up; Hope Ryden: 20 up; Medford Taylor: 12 up, 18 lo, 20 lo, 23 lo, 34 lo; Art Wolfe: 2 left, 6-7; Cary Wolinsky: 56 lo; Belinda Wright: 5 up, 11 lo; Shutterstock: Max Blain: 59 up.

For more information, please call 1-800-NGS-LINE (647-5463) or write to the following address:

NATIONAL GEOGRAPHIC SOCIETY
1145 17th Street N.W.
Washington, D.C. 20036-4688 U.S.A.

Visit the Society's Web site at www.nationalgeographic.com

Library of Congress Cataloging-in-Publication Data available on request
ISBN: 978-1-4263-0055-4

Printed in Belgium

Series design by Jim Hiscott.
The body text is set in Avenir; Knockout.
The display text is set in Matrix Script.

Front Cover—Top: Schoolchildren visit Sydney Opera House in Sydney Harbour; Low Far Left: Uluru at sunset; Low Left: A koala bear; Low Right: Aboriginal artist Terry Yumbulul paints sea creatures; Low Far Right: Lifeguards in Sydney

Page 1—Aboriginal boys with a laptop;
Icon image on spine, Contents page, and throughout: Decorated clapsticks

Produced through the worldwide resources of the National Geographic Society

John M. Fahey, Jr., *President and Chief Executive Officer;* Gilbert M. Grosvenor, *Chairman of the Board;* Nina D. Hoffman, *Executive Vice President, President of Book Publishing Group*

National Geographic Staff for this book

Nancy Laties Feresten, *Vice President, Editor-in-Chief of Children's Books*
Bea Jackson, *Director of Design and Illustration*
David M. Seager, *Art Director*
Priyanka Lamichhane, *Project Editor*
Lori Epstein, *Illustrations Editor*
Stacy Gold, Nadia Hughes, *Illustrations Research Editors*
Carl Mehler, *Director of Maps*
R. Gary Colbert, *Production Director*
Lewis R. Bassford, *Production Manager*
Maryclare Tracy, Nicole Elliott, *Manufacturing Managers*

Brown Reference Group plc. Staff for this Book

Volume Editor: Sally MacEachern
Designer: Dave Allen
Picture Manager: Becky Cox
Maps: Martin Darlinson
Artwork: Darren Awuah
Index: Kay Ollerenshaw
Senior Managing Editor: Tim Cooke
Design Manager: Sarah Williams
Children's Publisher: Anne O'Daly
Editorial Director: Lindsey Lowe

About the Author

KATE TURNER lives in London with her young family. She has worked in publishing for more than 15 years, during which time she has written widely for young readers, particularly about natural history and music.

About the Consultants

DR. ELAINE STRATFORD is head in the School of Geography and Environmental Studies at the University of Tasmania, and a senior lecturer working in the borderlands between cultural geography and political ecology. She has a particular interest in island studies. She has written about sustainability and globalization; environmental history, policy and politics; sense of place and community. Dr. Stratford is also the Coordinator of the Community, Place and Change theme area for the University of Tasmania, and on its Community Engagement Reference Group.

DR. J. M. POWELL is Emeritus Professor of Historical Geography at Monash University, Melbourne, Australia. His books and articles discuss aspects of the historical geography and environmental history of North America, Australia, New Zealand, and the wider British Empire. Currently, Professor Powell's major research and teaching interests concentrate on the history of geographical thought and on investigations into the relationships between changing appraisals of natural resources and the evolution of conservationism, environmental management, and pioneer settlement within the British Empire.

Time Line of
Australian History

B.C.

50,000s The first Aboriginal peoples reach Australia and spread throughout the mainland and Tasmania within 20,000 years.

ca 2500 The first dingoes arrive in Australia with seafarers from Asia.

A.D. 1600

1606 Dutch explorer William Jansz becomes the first European to see Australia.

1700

1770 James Cook, an English explorer, explores Australia's east coast and claims the continent for England.

1788 Captain Arthur Phillip brings 800 convicts to Botany Bay to begin colonizing Australia.

1789 Smallpox carried by colonists begins to kill the Aborigines as the colonists settle the continent.

1797 The first merino sheep are introduced; they will become the basis of Australia's wool industry.

1799 The Black War begins: Aboriginal people fight a six-year battle to protect their lands in the Hawkesbury and Parramatta areas of New South Wales.

1800

1817 "Australia" becomes the official name of the continent.

1836–7 A committee of the British House of Commons declares that the Aborigines have a "sacred right" to their land and condemns settlers' campaigns to take it.

1851 A gold rush begins in Victoria and New South Wales. Gold rushes throughout the 1850s lead to a doubling of the population and the arrival of many Chinese immigrants.

1856 Australia becomes the first country to use the secret ballot in its elections.

1860–1 Robert O'Hara Burke leads the first Europeans across Australia.

1890–7 Jandamarra, an Aboriginal resistance fighter, declares war on European colonists in West Kimberley and blocks settlement for six years.

1897 A law passed in Queensland limits where Aboriginal people can live and work and whom they can marry, and restricts their cultural rituals. It serves as the model for other restrictive laws.

1900

1901 On January 1, the Commonwealth of Australia comes into being.

1901 The new government passes the Immigration Restriction Act, commonly called the White Australia Policy. The act prevents the entry of non-European immigrants to Australia.

1902 The Franchise Act gives women the right to vote, but does not extend the right to Aboriginal peoples or people of Asian, African, and Pacific Island backgrounds.

1906 *The Story of the Kelly Gang*, made in Australia and the world's first feature-length film, premieres in Melbourne.